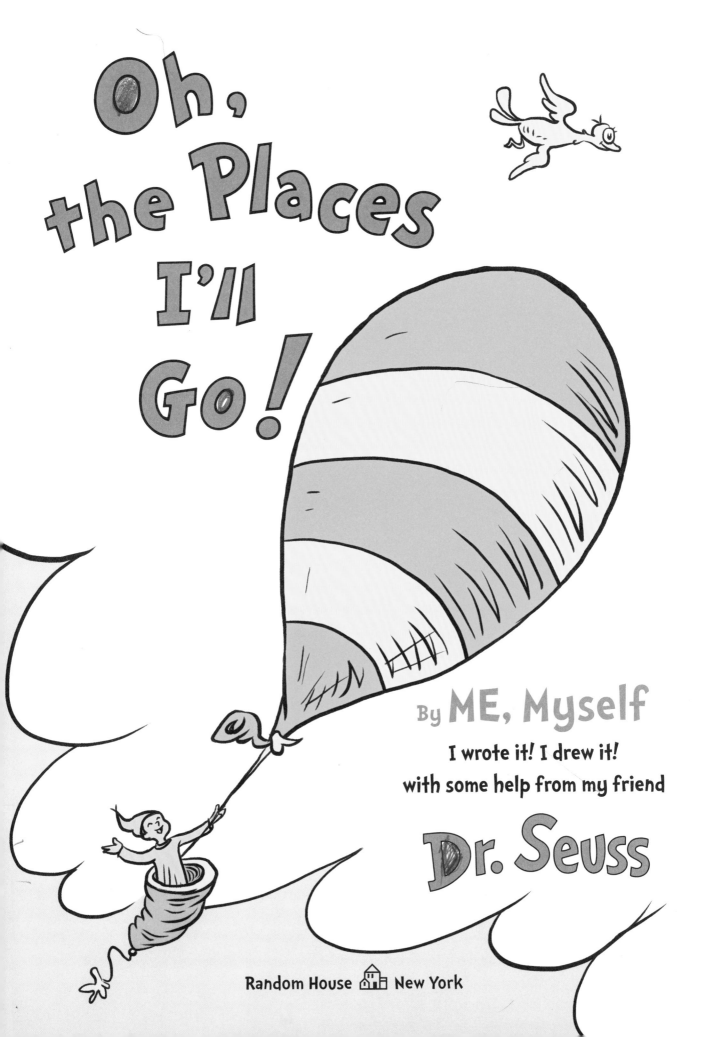

Oh, the Places I'll Go!

By ME, Myself

I wrote it! I drew it!
with some help from my friend

Dr. Seuss

Random House New York

Visit us on the Web!
Seussville.com
randomhousekids.com

Educators and librarians, for a variety of teaching tools, visit us at RHTeachersLibrarians.com

ISBN 978-0-553-52058-3

Library of Congress Control Number: 2014946571

Printed in the United States of America

10 9 8 7 6 5 4 3 2 1

Oh, the Places I'll Go!

Congratulations— to ME!

Today is my day.

Today is:

_____,
day of week

_____ _____ , _____
month   day   year

I'm off to Great Places!
I'm off and away!

Today is **special** because . . .

☐ I graduated from:

_____

☐ It is my birthday

I became a big brother/sister ☐

I learned something new ☐

Someone loves me ☐

I did this:

☐

I have brains in my head.
My head looks like this ↙

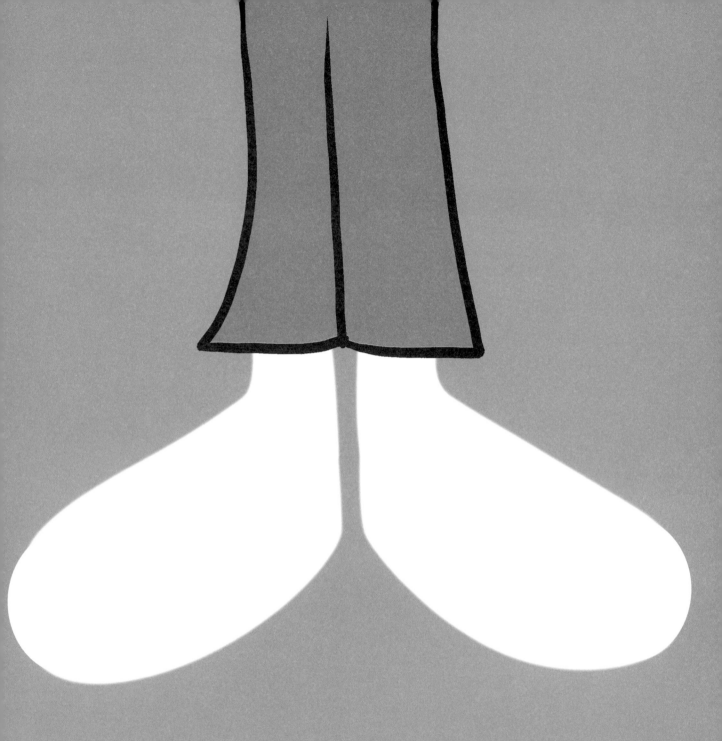

I have feet in my shoes.
My shoes look like this

I can steer myself
any direction
I choose.

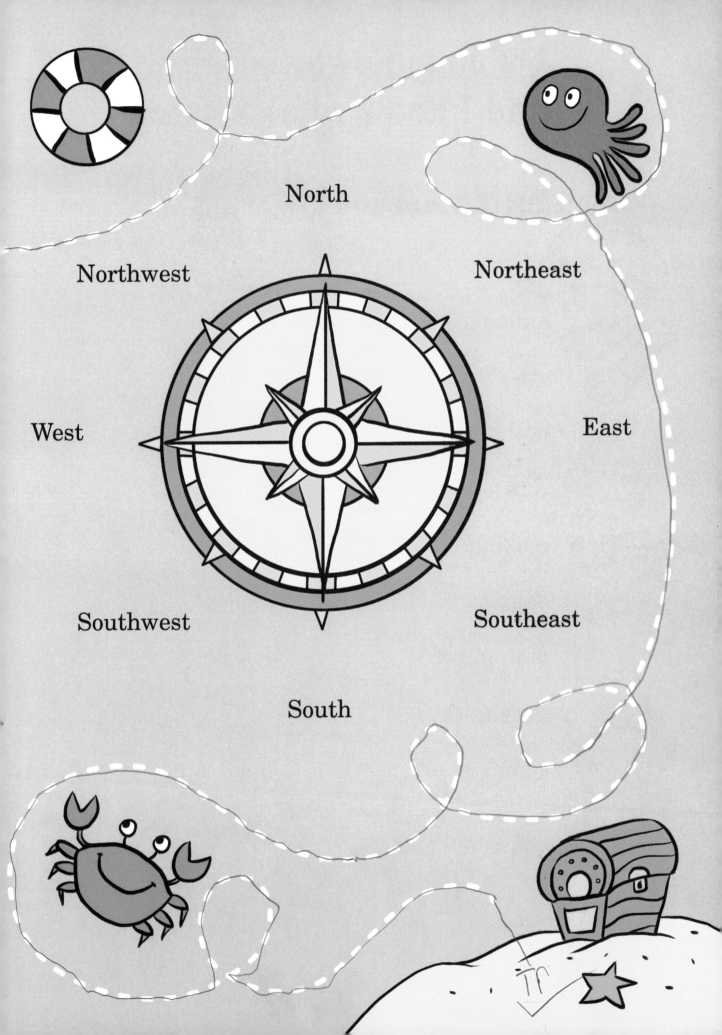

North

Northwest

Northeast

West

East

Southwest

Southeast

South

I'm on my own.
And I know what I know.

THIS is what I know about:

circle what you know about

animals	math
art	movies
books	music
cars	outer space
cooking	sports
dancing	superheroes
dinosaurs	toys
fairy tales	_____
games	and _____

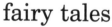

THIS is what I want to know MORE about:

animals	math
art	movies
books	music
cars	outer space
cooking	sports
dancing	superheroes
dinosaurs	toys
fairy tales	_____
games	and _____

And *I* am the one

Here are all the places I'll go:

airport	cousin's house
amusement park	elementary school
aunt's house	farm stand
babysitter's house	friend's house
bank	grandparents' house
barbershop	grocery store
beach	hair salon
bookstore	home
bowling alley	hospital
campgrounds	Kingdom of Didd
circus	lake

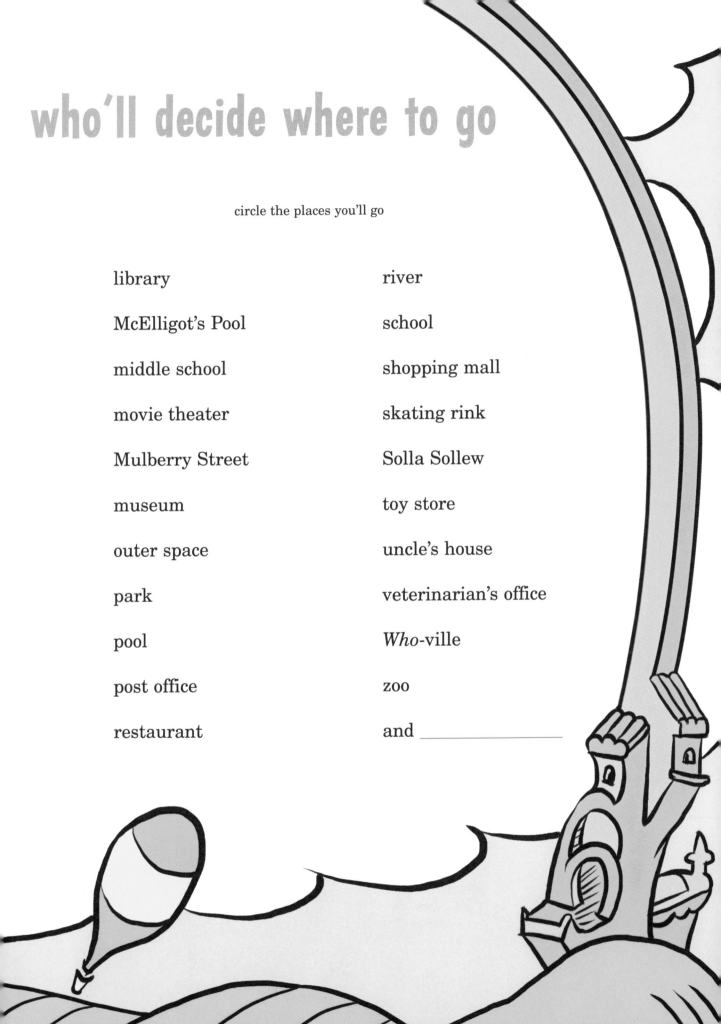

who'll decide where to go

circle the places you'll go

library	river
McElligot's Pool	school
middle school	shopping mall
movie theater	skating rink
Mulberry Street	Solla Sollew
museum	toy store
outer space	uncle's house
park	veterinarian's office
pool	*Who*-ville
post office	zoo
restaurant	and _____

Oh, the Places I'll Go!

I colored the states I want to visit.

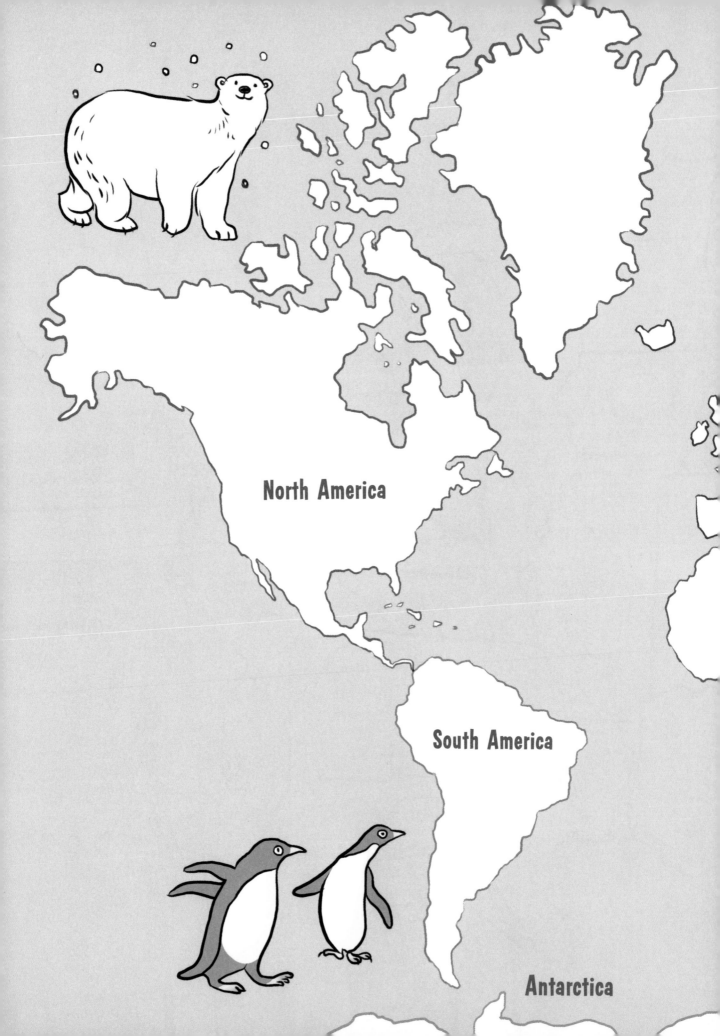

North America

South America

Antarctica

More Places I'll Go!

I colored the continents I want to visit.

Europe

Asia

Africa

Australia

And More Places I'll Go!

I colored the planets I want to visit.

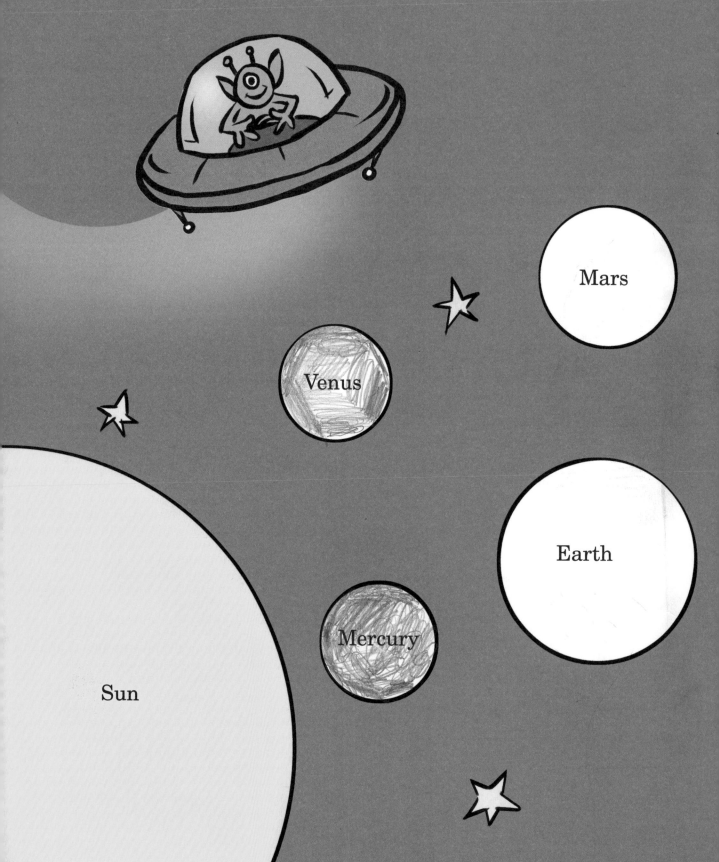

Not a planet, but I'd like to go there anyway!

Pluto

Uranus

Neptune

Jupiter

Saturn

I'll be on my way up!
I'll be seeing great sights!

Spaceship

Airplane

Tractor

Skis

My favorite way to travel

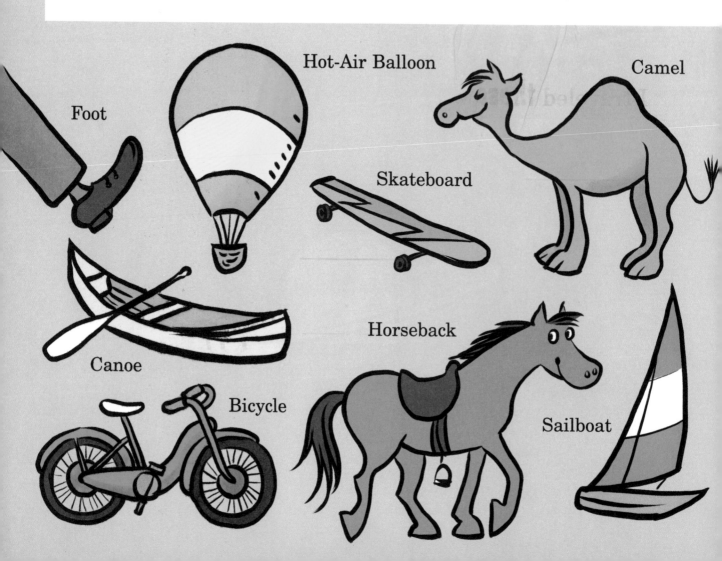

Foot

Hot-Air Balloon

Camel

Skateboard

Canoe

Horseback

Bicycle

Sailboat

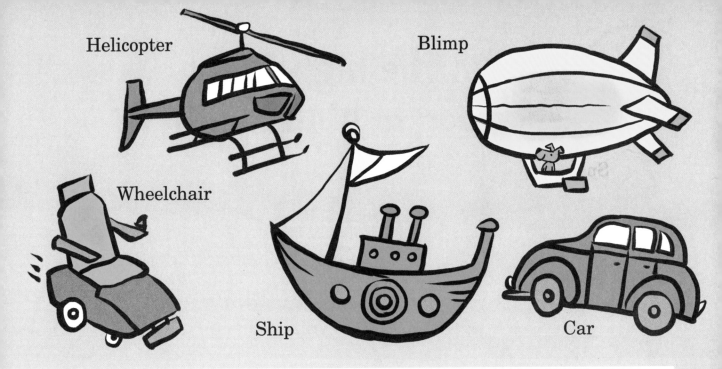

Helicopter

Blimp

Wheelchair

Ship

Car

is by: _____

I traveled **these** ways:

_____

_____

_____

Train

Roller Skates

Unicycle

I'll join the high fliers
who soar to high heights.

If I had my own balloon, it would look like this!

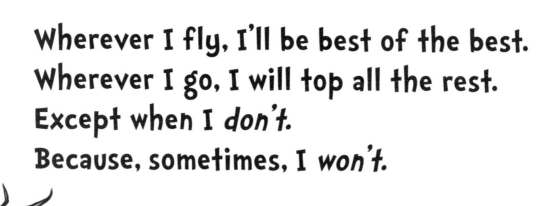

Wherever I fly, I'll be best of the best.
Wherever I go, I will top all the rest.
Except when I *don't.*
Because, sometimes, I *won't.*

When I grow up, I will be **BEST** at

_____

I will be **BEST** because

_____

I will be **SECOND BEST** at

_____

I will be **THIRD BEST** at

_____

I don't want to be **BEST** at

_____

START

I will come to a place
where the streets are not marked.
Some windows are lighted.
But mostly they're darked. . . .

FINISH

The Waiting Place . . .

No one dreams about waiting
But happen, it will.
And when I am WAITING,
I'll be standing still.

Things I am waiting for:

- [ ] my birthday
- [ ] a snow day
- [ ] a new pet

☐ my own room

☐ summer

☐ a bike

☐ a new tooth

☐ ice cream

☐ a visit from
the Cat in the Hat

☐ and _____

Somehow I'll escape
all that waiting and staying.
I'll find the bright places
where Boom Bands are playing.

When I grow up, I want to write a song called:

_____

I will play this instrument:

_____

I might even invent an instrument called:

_____

Here's what it would look like ↓

And when I'm in a Slump,
I'm not in for much fun.
Un-slumping myself
is not easily done.

Six Ways I Will Un-slump Myself

1. Read this book!

2. _____

3. _____

4. _____

5. _____

6. _____

With banner flip-flapping,
once more I'll ride high!
Ready for anything under the sky.

My banner looks like this

I may go far, but of all the **places** I'll go,
the places I'll always love MOST are:

And the **people** I'll want with me are:

Oh, the places I'll go!
There is fun to be done!
There are points to be scored.
There are games to be won.

When I grow up, I will:

☐ play lots of sports

☐ play some sports

☐ never play sports

When I grow up, I will play these games:

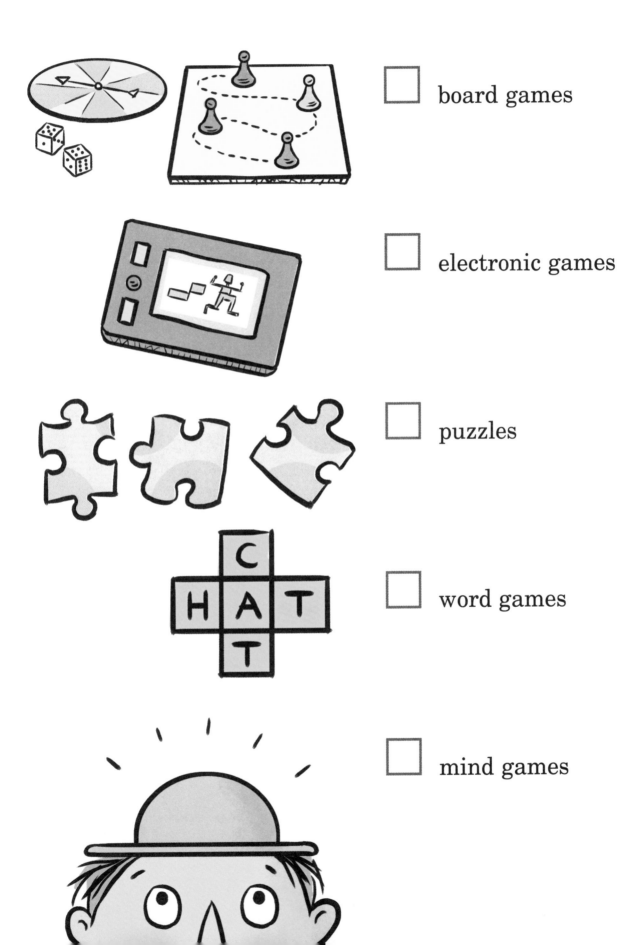

☐ board games

☐ electronic games

☐ puzzles

☐ word games

☐ mind games

Fame! I'll be famous
as famous can be,
with the whole wide world
watching me win on TV.

These are things
I will be famous for:

_____

_____

_____

_____

These are things
I will NOT be famous for:

_____

_____

_____

_____

I won't be stopped.

Onward up many
a frightening creek,
though my arms may get sore
and my sneakers may leak.

I will GO ON!

START

FINISH

On and on I will hike.
And I know I'll hike far
and face up to my problems
whatever they are.

Here's where I would like to hike:

in the desert

over snow and ice

in the woods

in a city

And will I succeed?
Yes! I will, indeed!
(98 and ³/₄ percent guaranteed.)

Some advice I've gotten from . . .

a parent:

_____

_____

_____

a grandparent:

_____

_____

_____

a teacher:

_____

_____

_____

a relative:

_____

_____

_____

a family friend:

_____

_____

_____

I'LL MOVE MOUNTAINS!

I will move mountains by:

- ☐ building things

- ☐ fixing things

- ☐ discovering things

- ☐ creating things

- ☐ performing things

- ☐ _____

- ☐ and _____

Plus, I will move mountains by helping:

☐ kids

☐ animals

☐ people

☐ the Earth

☐ outer space

Today is my day!
My mountain is waiting.

Here's my mountain

I'm off on my way!

When I grow up, I want to

_____

I want to because

_____

_____

_____

_____

_____

_____

_____

_____

_____

_____

_____

_____

_____

_____

_____

_____

_____

_____

_____

paste
your
picture
here

By ME, Myself

_____
name

These are the signatures of the people who will help me on my way to the places I'll go!

_____ _____

_____ _____

_____ _____

_____ _____

_____ _____

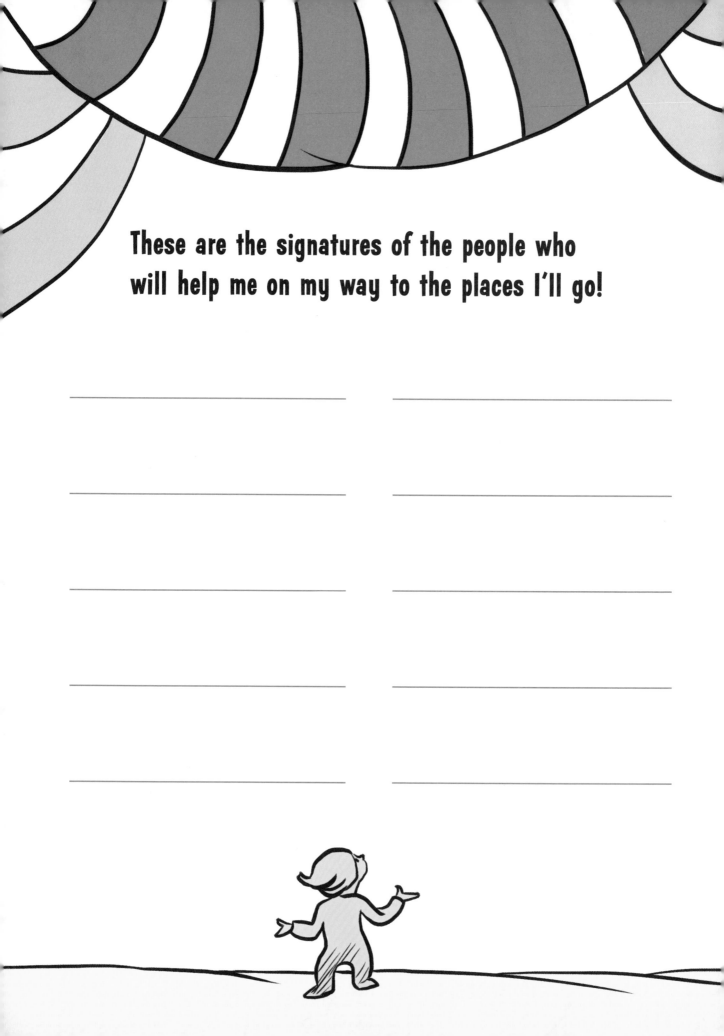

_____   _____

_____   _____

_____   _____

_____   _____

_____   _____

tasha

POSTCARD

Today Is
My Day!

FROM:

TO: